THE SPIRIT OF RHYME

Edited by

Heather Killingray

First published in Great Britain in 2001 by
POETRY NOW
Remus House,
Coltsfoot Drive,
Peterborough, PE2 9JX
Telephone (01733) 898101
Fax (01733) 313524

HB ISBN 0 75432 628 4
SB ISBN 0 75432 629 2

FOREWORD

Although we are a nation of poets we are accused of not reading poetry, or buying poetry books. After many years of listening to the incessant gripes of poetry publishers, I can only assume that the books they publish, in general, are books that most people do not want to read.

Poetry should not be obscure, introverted, and as cryptic as a crossword puzzle: it is the poet's duty to reach out and embrace the world.

The world owes the poet nothing and we should not be expected to dig and delve into a rambling discourse searching for some inner meaning.

The reason we write poetry (and almost all of us do) is because we want to communicate: an ideal; an idea; or a specific feeling. Poetry is as essential in communication, as a letter; a radio; a telephone, and the main criterion for selecting the poems in this anthology is very simple: they communicate.

CONTENTS

THE NOMAD

The nomad no home had, apart from his tent,
Of goatskin and willow cane, skilfully bent,
And finally fastened with stout goatskin thread
(Goatskins he used for his blankets and bed)
Light as a snowdrift, yet strong enough to withstand
The rough winter winds which bite through the land.
His footwear is sandals, from the rough leather cast
With thongs long as dog leads, and made strong, to last.

The nomad's a loner, a mankind disowner,
He follows the wanderings of his much loved flock,
While they're grazing he guards them
                with his eye and his crook
Or while browsing the verges of woodland and brook
No fearsome beast, nor fowl of the air
May attack or maraud them while the nomad is there.
When dusk approaches and stars gleam in the sky -
The goats chew their cud, happy heave of a sigh,
The nomad gathers kindling, his fire is alight,
Stirs his stew pot with pleasure and welcomes the night.

The nomad no home had, apart from his tent.

Jane Finlayson

A POET GOES SHOPPING

I went to the shops, a few days ago
Just to buy a loaf of brown bread.
Inspirational thoughts flashed into my mind
And two lines got stuck in my head.

With basket in hand, I raced down the aisle
Still trying to hold onto the words
Reciting the lines as I picked up the bread
Not conscious that anyone heard.

Whilst others were pondering their shopping lists
And debating what was for tea
I rehearsed aloud, the words in my head
And all eyes were looking at me.

I stood by the fridge, frozen peas still in hand
When the next bit of verse came along.
So delighted was I, as the words flowed like wine
Never noticed anything wrong.

Gliding still on, with dreams of my head,
Of becoming the next Poet Laureate
And that tall man appeared, to present me my prize
It was *me!* The Poet who'd won it!

The man, unconvinced, though I tried to explain
Genius thought had led me astray.
He thought I was mad, that words in my head,
Had made me forgotten to pay.

When the police were called in, I died with shame.
'It's all a mistake I can pay!'
But everyone smiled and smirked to themselves
As they led that 'mad poet' away.

Next week, I'm in court, on a shoplifting charge
And in verse I'll explain to the Beak
That genius like mine, just cannot conform.
(And hope he's a 'poetry freak'!)

Patricia Powell

GOD IS ENOUGH

('Blessed are they who mourn for they shall be comforted'
Matthew 5 verse 4)

God is enough to meet your need in sorrow
He is enough to bring you through tomorrow
God is enough 'tis He who draws 'the plans'
God is enough; He holds us in his arms.

God is enough, when we put our trust in *Him*
He is enough, when our eyes with tears are dim
God is enough as tougher gets life's way
'The Morning Star' - He lightens each new day.

Beth Stewart

THE CHILDREN

The children today certainly go to school
but quite often some of them break the rule.
The teachers must not give them a little smack any day
when we were young we were smacked anyway.

If we were naughty in school any day
we were sure to have the cane anyway.
It often made us really behave
even if we thought we were brave.

Now even the parents have to take care every day
whatever the children are up to anyway.
If a child gets a little smack on its bot
sometimes someone reports it on the spot.

It's hard on the parents any day
for doing just a little smacky anyway
and another thing, children shouldn't give the cheek
like they often do to people they meet in the street.

The good children suffer because of this anyway
the naughty ones treat them nasty every day.
It's really not fair on the good children today
that the naughty ones get away with it anyway.

Who'd be a teacher today anyway
even if they have lots of good children anyway.
Some children love their teachers there's no doubt
but others are naughty and will shout.

So think of the old days when we were in school
we were punished if we broke a rule.
A teacher today has no standing at all anyway
It's a wonder that people take it up today.

Kay Taylor

FENLAND FAYRE

A vast expanse of clear-blue sky,
Cotton-wool clouds rising high;
Above the wind - a curlew's cry,
Skylarks to the heavens fly.

Water in the dykes run slow,
Tall reeds on their deep banks grow;
Willows sprouting green leaves bow,
Stately swans are nesting now.

Daffodils with trumpets gold,
Tulips, red and pink stand bold;
Fields of beans, their perfume sweet,
Strawberry-teas - a summer treat!

Windmills' sails go creaking round.
Across the fields, sweet church bells sound
With towers square and steeples tall
Pointing heavenwards, call us all!

Maggie Smith

AD' INFINITUM

We've all seen the commercials that appear on our TVs
And though some are quite awful, there are often those that please.
Like all the cartoon characters and clever animations
And talking chimps, dressed up and set in funny situations.

The argument still rages on whose bacon is the leanest
And to this day I still don't know whose powder washes cleanest!
They try to sell us anything from oven chips to cars.
I'm sure if it were possible they'd sell us trips to Mars!

On long, dark winter evenings travel agents find it pays
To show us scenes upon our screens of summer holidays.
But when we've bought the Christmas treats and poverty prevails
We're pestered by the adverts for the January sales.

Some argue that the adverts interrupt a programme's flow
And should be done away with and they may be right although
I find that the commercial breaks mean just one thing to me;
A perfect opportunity to make a cup of tea!

Dennis Turner

EVERLASTING LOVE

I wish that I could hold you close, and your dear face I still could see.
That I could feel your arms around me, and know your smile was just
for me
Yet your love for me was in your eyes, but not for me alone,
For in those precious moments, you had caught a glimpse of home.

It's very hard for me to know, that it's time for you to go.
The heartache that I feel within, I know I must not show.
For we know that God had given us, a time to share our love,
But now he needs you close to him, in his heavenly home above.

So may God bless and keep you dear, as he takes you in his arms,
Let him soothe away the pain, and give you peace that gently calms.
For my love will ever be with you, and you'll always be in my heart.
So go to him in peace my dear, for we'll never be apart.

June Margaret Avery

THE WALL

A dry stone dyke offers little cheer,
but its greyness protects as the sheep nestle near.
Lichen covered and centuries old,
still standing guard after the sheep are sold.
And in the summer it also protects,
although not seen and crumbling with neglect.
withstanding searing summers and winters pall,
aloof and quiet and colourless . . . the wall.

Joe Waterman

THE EYE OF THE BEHOLDER

Don't pity the man with irregular features;
Such creatures succeed with the opposite sex;
Women aren't vexed by a plain honest treasure;
A measure of kindness, some humour he shares;
They're glad to know that man on the phone is
No selfish Adonis, but someone who cares.

Leo Taylor

PROGRESS

When I was young my talents were few
But as I got older my talents grew
So varied are they now with poetry
and painting
Computing and dancing,
and swimming I like to do

Is it a talent or a hobby you may be
the judge
It takes me out of myself and makes
me budge
I guess it's because I now have
the time
To spend how I like be it painting
or rhyme.

Audrey Allott

GARDEN PESTS

Stung by a wasp,
Bitten by a flea,
Pierced by a mosquito,
They all adore me.

I don't like the bites,
The swellings, the stings,
The soreness and the itches,
And the way the Dettol pings.

The flesh must be succulent,
The flavour divine
To these pests which overpopulate
The garden I call mine.

Kathleen Goodwin

MY BIRTHDAY

Fifty-two I am,
A funny age to be
Each morning when I wake
I'm only twenty-three
Today is an exception
I'm feeling ninety-nine
So this could be the reason
I wrote this silly rhyme.

E Torkington

JUSTIFY

Can you justify you choose to believe
they don't think or feel or grieve
when you kill them for their skin
or steal their liveness from their fin
or murder them so you can eat
their bodies as a pile of meat?

What of three basic rights within the Law
whether with scales, fin, feet or claw?
A right to the life, that is ours alone
Freedom with our own kind to roam
None subject to experiment.
And all should wail with loud lament
at those who fail to understand
none should suffer by man's hand

where do bounds of human mortality lie
in being instrumental for them to die?

When man steals a Sentient Being's breath
he hastens whose - but his own Death

Anita Richards

FAERIE SLUMBERS

I see faeries flutter round the ceiling
When I get that sleepy feeling,
And dreams come stealing over me like clouds;
Sprinkling pixie-dust into my eyes so weary,
I gaze on sights quite eerie,
Lights a-flickering in hosts of faerie crowds.
Casting ghastly shades of green and red,
Passing right above my bed
Whizzing back and forth, busy while they play;
Flitting everywhere like firework sparks,
Painting pictures in the dark,
Sombre shadows smiling at ones so fey.
Once, twice and thrice again, the sprites
Bathe the room in gleaming lights,
Or am I dreaming, when I watch them flicker by?
As lanterns shed a phantom lustre,
Faeries spread their wings and cluster;
Puffs of glitter dust sprinkle in my eye.
They crowd above and swoop towards me like butterflies
And purr their drowsy lullabies
In harmony with tiny humming wings a-blur;
Brushing past my face upon the pillow,
As bursts of colour billow
Bright cascading lights awaken dreams to stir.
Dancing right before my slumbers
In ever growing numbers,
The faerie folk are sowing sleepy thoughts,
That cloak the mind with wonder
And spells I fall under -
On the wings of owls, I fly to faerie courts.

Jonathan Goodwin

THIS TIME LAST YEAR

It seems my world is falling down, I can't believe how much I've cried.
Every thought I've had has been of you, it's nearly a year to the day
you died.
I didn't know it would be this hard, I thought I'd left the worst behind,
But the memories of this time last year are always on my mind.
I'm living through it all again, my heart feels fit to break,
The hurt I feel inside won't go, how much can one heart take?
Yet when I stand beside your grave, I know I shall be strong,
For inside each one of us you loved, your memory lingers on.

Melanie Elphick

WHERE?

There is a wee line sure 'tis divine,
I am my mate's and he is mine,
Here is how you know the sign,
His fingers like the weaving vine,
Pulse excitement in your spine,
Warming your innards as goblets of wine.

Be it on the mighty Rhine,
Or the murky waters of the Tyne,
The intensity of meeting eyes shine,
Tell the obvious story every time,
Hearts unite in the lover's rhyme,
I am yours and you are mine.

Even when the years decline,
Or loved one in another clime,
Never do forget to dine,
For heart's love does entwine,
Faith's clock which ne'er forgets to chime,
I am my love's and he is mine.

Anne Mary McMullan

FACTS ABOUT MONEY

There are people every day who complain they have no money
And they do not consider that one bit funny
They stand or sit in their jobs every day
Wishing and wanting to get more pay
If only some of them were not so dense
And just had some common-sense
Just to get their priorities with money right
Whether they are spending it during the day or at night

Before you go out shopping on any day
Always take note of the amount of your take home pay
Only purchase what you will need
Do not be caught in the trap of greed
If you bought all you think you could afford or can see
You may not realise how hard life for you could be
Be careful with money and you will be wise
Because you will then not end up in debt to your eyes

A faithful friend's love could not be bought
With any amount of money a person may have got
The best things in life for everybody are free
Which some people in this world are able to see
A priceless example is good health
Which is far more important than a person's wealth
Money can be useful in many a way
But it will not buy anybody happiness every day

Robert Doherty

BLAST-FURNACE

Roaming veils, distant hills,
Shadows cloaking rolling mills.
Dockland cranes, seaboard boundary,
Siliceous sands, casting foundary.

Primeval colours, spasmodic glows,
Urban landscape time bestows.
Titan structure, reddened sky,
Bellowing smoke, rasping sigh.

Encrusted casing, pungent air,
Excited embers, dragon's lair.
Brick, coke, smelting ore,
Heated blasts, vehement roar.

Centrepiece forbidding tower,
Vulcan's realm, awesome power.
Violent magma, inner purge,
Flames, sparks, robustuous surge.

Channelled path, moulded clay,
Broken dams, guided way.
Searing heat, reflected light,
Molten flows, luciferous bright.

Laurence Idell

IN PRAISE OF BEAUTY

I respond to the call to rhyme with pleasure: it is my duty
to celebrate some forms and shapes of beauty.
Though my attempt is motivated by zest,
I am afraid, my poem will not be the best.

The white peaks of Mont Rosa blush under the rising sun's ardour
and for a few instants glow with splendour,
but darkness shrouds mountains and sky
when the fog obliterates everything with its thick ply.

My sunny island emerges from the ever-changing sea
that from childhood has continuously allured me.
In this crowded town there is a secluded spot
dear to me: it helps me to balance troubles and be happy with my lot.

At the bottom of our garden quiet beauty can be found,
there is a pond hedged by a thick wood muffling any sound.
I sit in this spot wrought by hands and seasons
and wonder at the hidden roots of our personal history and its reasons.

I look at the pond and its banks decked with flowers
and I become more aware of the enduring strength of our powers
and as I conjure up unending space and past seasons with my eye,
I celebrate this that is, alive and now, under the same sky.

A Matheson

REMBRANDT BY HIMSELF

With loaded paintbrush poised you half-turn, dressed
In working clothes and take me by surprise;
Foiling my sly approach. You, unimpressed,
Observe me with your mild, impassive eyes.
An unforeseen communion, this, we share
As I intrude into your daily toil.
But, for a moment, we breathe the same air,
Essence of turpentine and linseed oil
Whose alchemy with pigments rare or base,
Directed by your skilful hand, resolves
Itself to art's illusion of your face.
Draw close and art ethereally dissolves
Back to the substance that preserves your fame;
Though every measured stroke proclaims your name.

Terry Edwards

WINTER BUTTERFLIES

When winter sun from winter skies,
shines down on winter butterflies,
my heart towards the summer springs,
and flutters with their velvet wings.
Dark crimson, yellow, mauve and white,
they shimmer in the silver light.
Their petals bunched like satin hems
ripple round their slender stems.
If only time would stay its course,
and let them dance among the stars.

They quiver when the west wind blows,
like ballerinas on their toes.
For as each season lives it dies,
and soon the dancing butterflies,
will lose their petals, drop their heads,
and wither in their dark green beds.
And we who watch their sad decline,
a few short paces down the line,
with faltering steps, and failing breath,
will join them in their dance of death.

AKS Shaw

FORECAST

Tears fell for the pain,
As I looked through the weeping glass,
At endless unremitting rain
For days and hours that plodding pass.

Would sunshine then have brought some cheer,
Or might it be callous, brittle,
A shallow, thoughtless, bright veneer,
That underlying cares belittle?

Tears that from the sky fall down
Wash away the sun's piled dust.
Moisture from the clouds' grey frown,
Seeps into the earth's baked crust.

Its weeping will bring out the green,
Dress nature in a rainbow coat -
Will such pleasure when they're seen
Ease the aching in my throat?

Passing time perhaps will bring
A lifting of this hurtful shroud.,
Will I one day enjoy the spring,
Emerge from my enveloping cloud?

Di Bagshawe

REFLECTIONS

In poppy fields, where I lay dying,
I turned to see my best pal crying.
In trenches deep the bodies heaped,
enough to make the strongest weep.

The blood laid red, in soil-like stream,
the noise of shell, and wounded scream.
Amongst the noise, a soldier's cry,
one more poor soul, that asked God why?

The guns they roared, was there no cease,
I turned, and my pal, dead in peace.

Tegid Furzer

NO GREATEST LOVE

Father in heaven
How can I express
The feelings that I have for you,
The love and thankfulness,
The joy of knowing Jesus Christ
As Saviour of my soul,
There is no greater love on earth
Than that which you have shown.
Your love has conquered all my fears,
And given me such peace.
My heart sings out with love for you,
My praise will never cease.

Audrey Coe

MODERNITY GIRL

Rounded bum, straining bust,
Rocking thighs, free from rust.
Shapely legs, limpid eyes,
Glistening lips, abnormally wise.
Trim from diet, the latest gear,
Waisting hem, fab for the year.
Front page of Vogue, centre of Man,
Hires out her bed, can open a can.
Always so trendy, discos and lights,
Inspiring hot breaths, she'll show you some sights.

The modernity girl, she must be all this,
Plastic and polish, computerised kiss.
To conform to the image, that is her task,
But what of her love, did nobody ask?

Vivian John Beedle

WHICH ROAD HOME?

Ann's man Stan
Said follow the van
And there should have been nothing to it
But they all looked the same
On the inside lane
She was lost before he knew it

Ann then found Dan
The removal man
And travelled up front in his cab
They took turns at driving
And seemed to be thriving
Ann thought this new life was fab

Then said Ann to Dan
You know that I can
Take control so much better than you
So be a good man
Please follow my van
And try not to get lost in the queue

This motorway madness
Had led to much sadness
Now Ann, Stan and Dan were alone
But then Dan met Holly
And life was quite jolly
For they both knew the way to get home

The moral of this little tale -
Is selfish people often fail
So please don't leave your faithful spouse
To walk behind and follow you
Avoid the A1 - and take the B2
You will find it leads to Happy House!

Tracy Palazzo

PROMISE OF SPRING

Star-like blossoms from the small trees stare
Beneath the daffodils are aware
The snowdrops also wish to share
The promise of spring

Though frost is still upon the grass
These late winter days soon will pass
Then spring will flaunt its joy en masse
When song birds sing

Roland Seager

THE ROOM

I must unlock a door, key to place
Decor gloom, stripped of grace
Cluttered, yet bare, of no object find,
Search! Reach further, opening mind.
Within cobwebbed corners jumbled oddments of thought,
Upon shelves of seclusion all emotion now sought.
I must shake off dust, wipe away grime,
Discover true feelings neglected through time,
Fit together all pieces, assemble as whole,
And with imagination furnish this room which is soul.

Philip Martin

THE MEETING

As I wait down at the station
For the train carrying my relation
I wonder if she's changed at all
Or if she's still slim and small.

Well here's the train at last I see
Now the moment of truth for me
Will she say 'You've grown quite fat'
Or is she too polite for that.

Here she is, she looks the same
I'm glad that we have met again
She smiles and says 'You do look good
You look much younger than you should.'

Now off we go to plan our week
Although the weather looks quite bleak
But we won't worry about that
We just want to sit and chat.

We'll spend the time reliving the days
Before we went our separate ways
The things we did, people we met
Thank goodness we have a whole week yet
To talk of times we'll never forget.

Pauline Nind

CANISTER

The past still holds me in its reigns,
yet I'm trying hard to become unchained.
Perhaps it's because I don't understand,
the path I'm taking, nothing's planned.
Or maybe it's the memories,
recurring, stronger,
in through dreams;
of days I've wasted,
moments lost,
and a childhood distant
still locked in a box.

Amy Phillips

THE WILD BELLS OF YOREDALE

Oh bells that arouse the village life,
To banish inertia, to cope with strife,
Urging good mortals go forth,
With music in their soul,
To cherish the love and comfort,
That dwells within their church and home.

So peal out wild bells in glorious sound,
And arouse the country wide,
Another millennium to conquer,
Let no man sleep or hide,
The world a happier place, we need to see,
Each in his own, can help it so to be.

J R Richardson

HOW BEAUTEOUS IS THE MORNING SUN

How beauteous is the morning sun, arising in the sky,
With myriad hues of pink and gold and a waking bird's first cry.
Then, soon, the birds unite to sing their symphony of praise,
No matter what the weather, they will do so all their days.
Their chorus so uplifting, like the angel choirs above,
Pouring out their sweetness to their Father, whom they love.
Oh, what rapture, oh what blessing, after darkness of the night,
Those little birds sing gratitude and sing with all their might.

God gave us lips to praise Him and hearts to share His love,
May we use them, to adore Him, our dear Father up above.
Oh, wake the ones, dear Father, who are sleeping in their sin,
May they open up their slumbering hearts and let the Saviour in.
Then, their lips will want to praise Him, like the dear sweet
singing birds,
And their hearts be filled with wonder and their mouths pour forth
sweet words.
No matter what the weather, be it wet or fine,
They will want to sing to Jesus, our dear Saviour divine.
No matter what their troubles, if the road seems hard and long,
He will fill their hearts with sunshine and their mouths with joyful song.

Winifred R Pettitt

33

WOLF MAN

I ran with the wolves at midnight,
A member of the pack,
Knowing that with the dawning
I must, alas go back.

Back to a world I hated,
Where I did not belong,
Trapped in a concrete jungle,
The call of the wild so strong.

Seeking our prey in the forest,
We coursed on silent feet,
Ready to kill and devour,
Any creature we might meet.

Fruitless our search till dawn came,
When I changed from wolf to man,
Snarling the pack chased after me,
So away from them I ran.

They followed closer and closer,
Till I could run no more,
As I turned to face them boldly,
I found myself on the floor.

As I gazed around in wonder,
It was my bedroom I saw:
Had I been merely dreaming?
Yet my feet were muddy and sore.

Margaret Bailey

LINDA

Linda was a special one
Her flame red hair shone like the sun
Her cheerful smile and friendly ways
Will remain in our hearts always
Wife, mother, daughter and grandmother
To be remembered as no other
This lovely lady, so young to go
Linda, we'll always love you so

Marie Housam

THE CHOKER

Pearly drops of fear
Growing, glistening as a tear
Trembling, tumbling from the brim
Salt its way below the chin
Choke young neck
With diamonds adeck
Adorn and warn

You'll never cry your cares away
Cup the drops, allay the flow
Deeply swim within
Faith supports
Crystallises future terse
Create surprises hence
Ah - your eyes are dry
May you wonder why.

Brenda Dove

A LATE REGRET

I want a son to carry on
The name my father bore
I want a son, who's big and strong
When I can live no more
It seemed to me, with all I've got
A fortune, house and fame
That all these things, one day will rot
Just leave behind my name.
I've never had these thoughts before
The urge to recreate
But suddenly I am forty-four
And I'm worried I'm too late
It's not that I regret my life
Ambition ruled my star
I had no time for home or wife
For I knew I could go far
How strange that something's missing
After all the things I've done
Somehow a fortune means much less
When you haven't got a son.

June Davies

CLOUD DEPTH

Field of wonder,
Up in open skies.
Who would want to be under;
Denied pleasure, without fees.

Touched by sensolli sun,
The heart fully won.
Silvery cloud of fortune;
Overcome by tapestry, fine tune.

And there, the smooth grey.
Peace, persuading journeying.
The soul, a willing prey;
Treatment, for the yearning.

Irresistible snow white,
Creative voice, of the emancipated.
Wonder never anticipated,
The heart lost, in exquisite bite.

And roared delight,
Arrows of fruit.
So much joy, in sight;
Wish, eternally, would be the root.

Heavy dark cloud,
The soul lamenting, world loud.
Appreciating, compassionate care;
Holy love, never leaving you, bare.

Believe, clouds full of fertile lessons.
If only we knew the language,
Feel, would be better persons;
Station, needing no salvage.

Rowland Warambwa

BEHIND THE MASK

Hidden facade, behind smiling mask
lost, lonely figure, desperately forlorn
gaunt body, huddling cold cellar steps
haunted face, haggard eyes shadow born

grim-coated bulb, offers solitary glow
dripping dank, monotonous lament of sadness
cracked mirror, pock-marked mocking
soulless smile reflected, staring madness

heavy shuffled feet, encroaching darkness
black, bleak portrait, tortured mind
dirt-grained chair, instrument of release
trembled hands gripping, dragging behind

rough oil-stained rope, softly threaded
rusted holding hook, embedded deep
flesh-filled noose, creaking splintered joist
cracked mirror, dark reflected visions leap

inner demons, seeking silent succour
jerking feet of dangled leg, fevered brain
scuffed shoes kicking, clattered chair
hard-tiled floor, shattered wooden grain

resting dampened waste and litter
final rasping breath escapes sighing silence
cracked mirror, revealing secret vision
twitching lifeless doll, suffered violence

Luke Thomas

A TINY SPECK OF WHITE

Sitting on the beach on a hot sunny day
Glancing at the idle ships anchored in the bay,
Suddenly on the horizon a tiny speck of white,
Caught my attention as it glistened in the light.
Slenderly and gracefully it came into my view,
Full sails billowing white against a sea of blue.
Fascinated I watched as it weaved its way around,
Masterly and skilfully over gentle waves it wound
I held my breath in excitement, my pulses beating out.
When racing into the wind again the craft was turned about,
I couldn't take my eyes away from such a splendid sight.
As it headed back to the horizon and became a tiny speck of white.

Rita M Arksey

FLYING TOWARDS SUNSET

Is this like dying Lord, this long-haul flight
Between two continents, two worlds apart
Sailing on puff-balls tinged with rosy light,
Peach-orange spars, fantastic iceberg art,
Pink castles, curving harbours, midnight seas,
A fairy kingdom steeped in evening sun!
Far distant are the dry acacia trees,
White-sanded shores where dark-eyed children run
On spice isle Zanzibar. Now swiftly on
Through looming darkness, yearning soon to be
Within the warm embrace once more of one
Whose love through life has been a rock for me,
Whose arms reach out, wherever I may roam.
Is dying Lord, like this, like coming home?

Kathy Butler

TEMPORA MUTANTUR

He was a friar of orders grey, but now, may God defend me,
He's thrown his old grey robe away; his dress is much more trendy
He'll dress to show that he's 'in touch', this fashion statement means
He wears T-shirts that cost too much, and smart designer jeans.

She was a nun to silence bound by a most solemn vow,
Then Rome changed everything around and you should see her now.
Her old guitar has been replaced by an electric bass.
She may still be both chaste and poor, but watch her set the pace.

He was a solitary monk who spurned both drink and grub.
Now he's the secretary of the 'Hermit's Social Club'.
They meet together every day, no more of isolation,
And drink to pass the time away, to hell with deprivation!

Bewildered lay-folk stand amazed at changed in our clerics.
The way they talk and act and dress would give the saints hysterics.
No more the pious, sombre clothes, like cassock or biretta,
For anything, it seems, now goes, the more extreme the better.

Oh! Let's bring back those golden days, when you could tell
                                        most clearly
Just who was who. Ah golden days! When clerics dressed severely.
Let's get back to a previous age before the rot began,
Endorse the saying of the age that clothes *do* make the man.

Terry Clifford

SKYLARK'S SONG

memory fade
longing still
lofted grass
stunted hill

drifted song
catching ear
hunting high
seeking near

remembered field
urging strong
lingered lost
skylark's song

childhood haunt
recalled thrill
prickled skin
summer chill

trampled corn
hazy days
timeless seams
wandered ways

drifting cloud
empty sky
drawing blank
haunted sigh

heated hours
stretching long
searching vain
skylark's song.

Paul Birkitt

MY LOVE FOR YOU

My love for you is newly born,
I think of you both night and morn.
I know life has its rose and thorn
But true love endures, 'tis never worn.

My love for you grows day by day,
I'm almost sure you feel the same way.
With your sweet smile to me you convey
A bright ray of hope, so I boldly say:

Agree to be mine, 'tis not sin or crime,
Life's strenuous ladder together we can climb
For I shall love you till the end of time
When my life's timepiece its last beat will chime.

Falling in love is a great adventure.
Every heart suffers that bittersweet torture,
And, when one knows how to care and nurture,
Love will keep fresh like a green pasture.

Alice Zamanian

THE UNDESIRABLE MAN

A diamond ring? No thank you
No! I don't want a red sports car.
Your generosity exceeds you
But this time you've gone too far.

So listen very carefully
As I'll say it only once.
Don't attempt to interrupt me
Don't indulge your silly stunts.

All you do I question
You're like a ship without a sail.
Suspicions are now confirmed
You trade the truth for fairytale.

You can't buy my moral values
Now, that type of girl I'm not.
Love, respect and also honesty
Are things I like a lot!

Debbie Montague

BLUEBELLS ON THE BREEZE

Daffodils and bluebells dance in the breeze,
All around the crystal clear trickling brook,
Contented birds sing in the morning sun,
I am compelled to take a look,

If only we could make time,
To realise and see the beauty in our midst,
Instead of chasing the clock and our fortunes,
Because there-in lies the twist,

Our fortunes once made,
Will allow us the time to bide,
And take in all that there is,
A time refound, a time once denied,

But for many sadly they fall along the way,
Never seeing with open eyes,
Bluebells on the breeze or the kingfisher's wing,
Or the beauty waiting under clear blue skies.

Too late for them to smell the fragrant rose,
Or watch the dawn creep across the bay,
Endless time is spent with noses to the grindstone,
Ample work filled hours, whittle away your days,

So remember your clock is ticking,
Your life's cycle, follows its course,
It is you and you alone who chooses to ignore,
Life's beauty and charm, and ever changing force,

So please take a long hard look,
At what is around you, what matters in your life,
Take a break, take a sabbatical,
Take a deep breathe, take a love, take a wife,

For there is far more to life than clocking on or off,
Or working from dawn to dusk or late into the night,
I challenge you to find time to sit and watch the stars,
On a cold clear evening, what a fantastic sight.

P J Littlefield

25P

When we reach the age of 80
Each week we get more, just 25p.
What do we do with such a sum
Dance a jig or sit on our bum.
Should we go mad on the booze
Buy a ticket for a world cruise
Give it to charity if we are kind
Panic buying won't be on our mind.
Wanting everyone to know
We're in the money, to let ourselves go.
It's all a dream, like rising damp
Won't even buy a 1st class stamp.
So what do we do with 25p
Blessed if I know, it's a problem to me.
A deposit for a walking stick
Just a thought! It makes me sick.
Mustn't think of buying a car
Don't think there's enough for a chocolate bar,
Not even a Mars bar or a Snickers
Certainly not socks or a pair of knickers.
80 years we wait for this
Isn't it wonderful, oh what bliss.
Then after the day our thoughts will be
Of when we were eligible for 25p.

Joan Jeffries

DAYDREAMER

Time stands peacefully still,
Submitting ideas as dreamers at will
Build visionary castles of copious desire,
Creating images built to inspire,
Allowing romantic ideas to take flight,
To laze in the warmth of utopian night
Deliciously free from normal routine
Sublimely sedated, calmly serene.

Designer of beauty ambitiously spread,
Quixotic visions dreamily read,
Extreme fabrication engages the trance,
Hypnotic conduction performing the dance,
To faraway places encrusted with gold,
Where fairy-tale characters never grow old.
Lost in the daydreamer's fantasy world,
Star-gazers bask in wonders unfurled,
Encased in a blanket of fanciful rhyme,
Lost in the dreamer's perception of time.

Josephine Duthie

DISTANCE ADORATION

She blessed me with her presence,
Yes, I felt her effervescence
Long before we started talking to each other.
Vivacious, but with grace,
Is never out of place,
And yes, I really believe that I love her.
Constantly around,
Her aura can be found
Anywhere that this dear woman's been.
Rainbows can't outshine
Lovely people when they're fine,
Especially this Lady, who I've seen.
So if I talk out loud
When I'm alone within a crowd
Ostracise me not, for I am thinking,
Remembering her charm,
This of course, to keep me warm
Her memory brings me pleasure in a twinkling!

Michael Kennedy

THE ENGLISH WEATHER

The weatherman forecasts conditions unsettled yet again
A dry bright start, followed by outbreaks of rain
Feeling really cool, well below the seasonal norm
Traditionally the spring weather should be quite warm

Cloudy and overcast, with many prolonged heavy showers
Risks of flooding in the south, over the next few hours
Sunny spells in the north, the outlook is mainly dry
Much broken cloud, with a chance of a blue sky

Summer is finally upon us, as temperatures start to soar
A heatwave like no other, this has never happened before
Many weeks so hot and dry, the likelihood of a drought
Has broken all the records, there isn't any doubt

Suddenly an eerie stillness, just a temporary lull
The clouds on the horizon are becoming very dull
Such a sultry feel, the atmosphere sticky and warm
Tonight there's every chance, of a localised summer storm

The heavens open wide, it's like stair rods coming down
Rain completely saturating, all the dry dusty ground
The sky is lit up, as the lightning starts to flash
The thunder rocks the earth, with a bang and a crash

Drifting into autumn, there's a distinct chill in the air
Strong winds and gales, stripping the countryside bare
Tonight dipping temperatures, possibly a ground frost
Gardeners' beware, delicate plants could be lost

Damp dark days ahead, with early morning mist
Dense fog in many places, these patches could persist
Icy stretches on roads, the cold wind doth blow
Tomorrow we could see, winter's first fall of snow

Linda Brown

FAIRIES

Do you believe in fairies,
So many people do.
Some have seen them in the garden,
And in the woodlands too.
In the glen they gently glide,
If they see you they will hide.
Dressed in emerald, silver and gold,
Fairy stories are always told.

So tiny and sweet with faces that gleam,
On the knoll they can be seen.
On the lily pond they float on leaves,
They like to sit upon your sleeves.
When there is a sudden breeze,
It's the fairies flying through the trees.
A toadstool is a shelter from the rain or sun,
They dance, play games and have lots of fun.

There are fire fairies, wind fairies,
Snow fairies too,
Pretty flower fairies with eyes of blue.
Is it make believe or is it true.
Are these little fairy folk
Living amongst me and you.

Carol Rees

BEEN THERE, DONE THAT!

Beware of 'should' and 'ought', for they will prove
Anathema, a curse untold,
Which counteracts the alchemy of love,
Which turns to lead the purity of gold.
As tarnish veils the metal's lustrous glow
So rectitude usurps affection's bloom.
Its moral obligation can bestow
A chill more unremitting than the tomb.
No sun, no joy in life, no stolen kiss,
No whispered love or unconsidered word;
No well-springs of delight, but merely this,
'Do not your wish, do only what you should'.

Enmeshed in duty, loveless, day by day,
Affection balks and, tearful, creeps away.

John Beazley

THE PAINTING

In a gallery in a foreign place
My heart throbbed at a faster pace
Captivated focusing on a famous face

His eyes held mine, as past him I walked
Saying far more than if we had talked
This artist was true to his own face, painted

On the canvas's using crazy colours with glaze
Did he realise the many nights and days?
His wounded expression in memory would stay

I recall the pained look and the bandaged ear
Immortalised on canvas sheltered from fear
Imprinted in my memory a soul so dear

In my room the old chair in France I found
The sunflowers grow tall outside in the ground
His kind of madness has entered my mind

Hunger and love fired his inspiration
Engrossed with these twin preoccupations
Women of today should take up painting.

Maisie Mattey

TIME

With what deep sorrow do I note the way
In which cruel Time - imperiously bold -
Relentlessly imposes, day by day,
His ravaged signature upon the old.
How sad to see youth's once smooth visage brought
To such a sagging, dry and sorry fate;
The skin that long ago was clear and taut
Now in its dismal grey and wrinkled state.
What grief to see the confident bright gaze
Shorn of its youthful lustre, now quite changed,
The brightness vanquished by a watery glaze,
The confidence for weakness now exchanged;
How bleak retreat of hair once lush and brown,
A bare expanse leaves, framed with wispy grey;
The lines of worry and the deep-etched frown,
The laughter lines erased, gone clean away.
Such dumb sights do of yet more changes speak,
The hesitant shamble, once thrusting stride.
Strong muscles grown now inelastic, weak,
So mere rising from a chair requires pride.

     Yet saddest of all, with mounting terror,
     All of this I see in my own mirror.

G F Pash

IN A HAPPIER TIME

The master writes the lines
With scratching chalk
His glare dismisses
All thought of talk.
I tried to find
His lines in a book
Turning musty pages
I took a look
But failed to find the lines
Written in a happier time.

Paul Wilkins

WELCOME TO MY WORLD OF POETRY

We must welcome the new dawn, as it spreads its daylight.
And at the close of a new day we must welcome the night.
For this sequence of events, is one of nature's trends.
That as a new day starts, then at nightfall it ends.

A day well lived will surely leave its mark.
So enjoy the sunshine in your life, and try to forget the dark.
A day lived in isolation, must truly remain the same.
But as a new day comes along, we have a chance to try again!

As we enjoy all of life's comforts, we must also expect the pain.
As we welcome the sunshine, we must also accept the rain.
As we appreciate all the good things, we must surely accept the bad.
And live with our disappointments, and pretend that we're rather glad.

For the pleasures of life can be a challenge, and often difficult too.
For all the good things in life carry a penalty, in most of what we do.
We can have a good day out and enjoy lots of fun.
But we cannot lay in bed as well, it simply can't be done.

Anticipation is greater than realisation, or so we are lead to believe
And what is realised tomorrow, has gone and can never be retrieved.
We must enjoy our moments of pleasure, and live out our every day.
Before that day is gone and lost forever, and swiftly swept away.

For we are given but a small measure, to take a taste of life as we will.
We must enjoy our taste of life as we find it, for we cannot expect
a refill.
The pleasures of life must be taken, and savoured like a glass of
fine wine.
Because life has imposed its restrictions, the restrictions of
limited time.

Charlie Walker

STIFF UPPER LIP!

We poets are a funny lot.
We think out rhymes, which down we jot,
On scraps of paper, until we might
Work on them, and laid out right.

It's not our way to be dejected,
If our work has been rejected.
There's no point in feeling blue,
Failure simply will not do.

We will sit and rethink out
What the poem's all about.
Change some words, rescan a line,
'Til we're happy that the content's fine.

So if you get a rejection slip
Remember, no quiver upon the lip.
Don't throw a tantrum, scream or cry.
Write some more, have another try.

John David Sams

THE GREY LADY OF GAYWOOD

There still stands the old manor house in Gaywood
Up the top alongside the clock
Now camouflaged by several small shops
Where the grey lady still walks through
The shutters and bolted doors.

It's built up around now with council estates,
Supermarkets and takeaway stores,
No one ever sees the grey lady, of
Long, long ago as she strolls along
Her meadows where once cowslips did grow
No hustle and bustle of this present life.

But to her ladies and gentlemen
Horses carriages and penny farthing bikes
Big hats, crinoline dresses
Hair in long tresses,
No takeaway shops, no curry breeze
A place of beauty everything at ease
Through the ages the grey lady
Of Gaywood will walk to visit her past,
She never stops for a curry
She never talks
She just strolls by thinking of days gone
Happy times, green meadows and the
Birds' sweet song.

The old house to the grey lady
Will ever remain
She will walk home to Gaywood again and again
So each night she will travel
From her churchyard grave
To her home which I hope
The National Trust will
Always save.

Kathleen Gilboy

QUESTIONS

How long is life?
I have a wife trouble and strife,
When shall we be dead and gone?
Will we be remembered long?
Sung of in song,
Is there an answer?

K M Clemo

PERHAPS A GIFT

If my inspiration come from above
Don't mean I got a gift
To write the words of love,

Just got to have a feeling
Deep inside your heart
Then it will happen
And the words will start.

So to write these words
That I put down for you
It ain't so funny
And that I know is true.

But it's something that I got
And it's something that I do
So if you call this a gift
Then I'll believe it from you.

Karen Anthony

Spirit Of The heart

Immortal spirit of the heart
What inspirations you impart
When half asleep and half awake
In-roads into my mind you make

To grasp and keep such glorious thought
Must not be lost, counted for nought
Precious fleeting words must never
Slip away, be lost forever

It is with pain poets give birth
To immortal lines of living verse
Fine lines like theirs are for sure
Destined to live forever more.

So here's to you poetic brothers
Greatest of gifts you leave for others
That they might be inspired too
To catch a fleeting gem or two.

Norah Page

THE COUNTRYSIDE

When I'm alone in the countryside I become a silent man,
I walk quietly in the shadows and keep hidden when I can.
I become one with the hawk and swallow, hunters in the sky,
I roam with the foxes, patrolling places where the rabbits lie.

I have sang with the dawn chorus and whistled with the lark,
I've seen things you wouldn't believe, in God's great country park.
There are spiders' webs on a dewy morn, like a misty carpet on
                                    the land,
Poppies dotted in the cornfields, as though sown by an unseen hand.

Now there's a deer, it's watching me, to it I'm not a threat,
I often spy the elusive badger, emerging from its set.
Gone is any longing for the city, give me the fields and the open air
And if you walk quietly in the shadows, you may find me
                                    sitting there . . .

Brian Ducker

AUTUMN

How great the soul of the sad sad air
The wind that plays such a mournful air,
The breeze is light and gently stirs
Rustling leaves and lofty firs.

Autumn's here and day must rest
From summer's blithe and loving quest
One must not care for the sad sad air
Nor leaves to leave a tree so bare.

Evening shadows hide the day
Of man's dour work, and children's play,
The darkness shrouds what would appear
And leaves are falling here and there.

Leaves that danced in the morning sun
Glistening, green, alive and fun,
Clothing the wood, bush and wall
From joyful spring until the fall.

Leaves that dressed the summer scene
Of blessed nature, merry, green,
Are now departing to their rest,
Summer's gone, the land undressed.

John M Carr

THE FAIRHAM NATURE RESERVE

Crystal clear the water fast flows
Past the grass bank on which I now rest
Fish swim effortlessly against the current
Moorhens jealously guard hidden nest
Reed that grows to the water's edge
Conceal weasel, vole, and stoat
Kingfisher dives in relentless search
Competes with anglers bright bobbing float

I see flower and fauna of all types and hue
And it fills my heart with such joy
For I thought scenes like this were a thing of the past
Distant memories of when I was a boy
But people who care have fought for the right
To protect, to farm, and preserve
This sight of such beauty for all eyes to see
In the Fairham Brook Nature Reserve

My gratitude goes to those who protect
They are the custodians of all I now see
Who tirelessly work to right years of neglect
And leave their mark on each grass, shrub, and tree
Their reward though not asked for is not monetary gain
Finding more pleasure in a reed warbler's song
Or the thrill of a brand new sighting
Of a species that was considered long gone

To hear the song of the nightingale
The woodpecker attracting a mate
Or catch a glimpse of a harvest mouse
These things we must save before it's too late
Yes, for those workers our pleasure is their business
To show us the joy of the countryside
They only ask for our consideration
And that we view all our landscape with pride.

Don Woods

65

LEAVE THE WASHING ON THE LINE

Let it dance,
Let it swing,
Let it stay,
Don't bring it in.
Let the wind
Enjoy a flirt
Blowing through
The lady's skirt.
Let the sleeves
And bright towels flap
And the peg fall out
Of the shapeless cap.
Let the hankies
Hang in rows
And enjoy a change
From wiping Fred's nose.
Let the woolies
Have a fling
And shoot higher
Than the rusty swing.
They've only kept
Their elders warm,
Not known the fun
Of getting torn.
Let those tights
Really fly
And step upon the clouded sky.

Let those clothes have some fun,
They've done no harm to anyone.

Gloria Thorne

ODE TO ALISON

Her beauty makes the angels weep
But she comes here to clean and sweep
She goes off into Jimmy's room
And starts with vacuum or a broom.

And there's no time to say her eyes
Are brighter than the stars that rise
Or with Venus and the Moon conspire
To fill the heavens with their fire.

Or that the mirrors of her soul,
Her eyes, must make the plants roll
Such power and beauty do they shine
From her sweet face of God's design

So everything we say's prosaic
I'd like to print a word mosaic
A portrait of a lady fair
In the few moments she is there.

But just as my words start to flow
She says that is time to go
And so my ode to Alison
Is never written, she has gone.

Phil McLynn

THE RAINBOW

The Rainbow arc that spans the sky
Is a beauty to behold
Whoever finds the end they say
Will find a pot of gold.

'Tis a promise in the heavens
Through sunshine after rain,
That God has given His children
That comes once more again.

The colours brightly shining
Set a seal upon the World
That God's love is ever present
Shown as the arc's unfurled.

The red is like the poppy fields
The orange like the sand
The yellow shineth as the sun
Green covers all the land.

Blue is like the 'circling' seas
Indigo the clouds
And violet gentle as a flower
That shouts God's grace aloud.

We have been given a promise here
'I set my bow in the cloud . . .
. . . A covenant between me and the earth'
This is what He vowed.

So we know now when we look to the skies
'Seed time and harvest shall not cease'
For all is calm when we lift our eyes
In the Rainbow which brings His peace.

Mollie D Earl

JONES THE SCRAP

Nothing was too big and nothing was too small.
Whatever 'twas you wanted, Jones the Scrap would have it all.
Mountains of scrap metal and stacks and stacks of wood,
Most of it was rubbish, but some of it quite good.

He'd weigh your lead and copper on scales he vowed were right,
But what you found heavy carrying, his scales made awf'lly light.
He'd haggle over pennies and count out every one,
And wouldn't dare look happy until you'd been and gone!

Railway trucks were loaded with scrap metal every day,
But the piles in Jones's scrapyard just *never* seemed to stray.
They just grew ever bigger, as dealers one and all
Brought in their loaded lorries to make the piles stay tall.

Jones's home life was quite different . . . everything was *new*,
A villa by the seaside, complete with wondrous view.
No expense was spared . . . he lived life to the full.
He ate and drank and smoked cigars all night without a lull!

His paunch grew ever bigger . . . his breath grew ever less.
He knew his current lifestyle had made his health a mess.
He was heading for the scrapheap - his ticker soon would cease.
It did! Poor Jonesy became another 'Rest in Peace'!

He found himself at Heaven, outside the Golden Gate,
Where St Peter took his name and told him where to wait.
'I'll have to go and ask if you're entitled to come in.
It all depends on whether you've led a life of sin!'

St Peter entered Heaven to discuss it with his Boss,
Who snorted, 'Jones the Scrap from Wales . . . I couldn't give a toss!
We'll have him if repentant . . . it isn't yet too late.'
But Jones had gone to his scrapyard . . . and so had the Golden Gate!

G K (Bill) Baker

MY LOVE POEM

I thought that I could never love anyone again
At the time it seems so great, until it all ends up in pain.
Yet when I'm in your arms I feel as time's stopped going by.
And when you have to leave I cannot bear to say goodbye
When we're not together I begin to lose my mind -
For it feels like an important part of me is left behind.
I think about your face, I hear your voice and see your smile.
And you seem so far away, I really miss you all the while.
You must think me as crazy going on and on this way,
But I love you and I think about you each and every day.
I would stay with you forever - yes forever and a year.
Please save me from a broken heart; don't ever disappear.

Nicola Chapman

LOVE IN '88

Love is an illusion,
Of feelings of confusion,
So here's a solution,
A two-hearted fusion,
Of a wonderful intrusion,
To an heavenly conclusion.

Amanda Jayne Biro

KEEP IT IN

Locked up tight within myself,
I store my troubles on a shelf.
It would be good to let them out,
To rant and rave and scream and shout.

But this I feel I cannot do,
For I could never burden you.
So, silently inside I'll keep
My problems bound and buried deep.

Suzanne Hicks

SHORT BREAK

Only yesterday, but a life-time away
In the late afternoon of a summer-like May
After an ecstatic hike across singing fields
They returned to the bedroom to change for a meal.

Moist and exhausted they flopped on the bed
Desiring each other, content to hold hands
Patient and certain of long life ahead
For loving and the promise of tomorrow's plans.

She kissed his cheek, he brushed her lips
With his as quietly they gave themselves up to sleep,
Two middle-aged lovers curled heart to head
One to sleep on, the cold sleep of the dead.

William Wood

THE SHROPSHIRE UNION CANAL

One of my favourite waterways
With tales to tell of bygone days,
The 'Shroppie's' gentle waters glide
Through Cheshire's lovely countryside.

Market towns are close at hand
Amid miles of farming land.
Canalside hostelries abound
And little shops are eas'ly found.

The locks are mostly a delight,
Especially the Audlem flight.
They are tended with such care
By the friendly keepers there.

Through field and village, rain and sun,
The pleasure boats cruise, one by one,
But this canal has memories clear
Of working boats from yesteryear.

Dawn Rickatson

ON THE EDGE

Do I take a step forward, or take a step back,
Do I take the easy way or face the 'flack'?
Am I strong enough to stand on my own?
Or do I live in fear of being alone?
As I take these pills I know it is wrong -
But I want to be somewhere I feel I belong.
My ghosts won't let go and my closet is full,
I no longer feel I am able to pull
Away from the edge that is beckoning me
I want to 'go over' - I need to be free.
I can no longer go on fighting alone,
My soul has been beaten too often, and thrown
Out into the gutter, out in the rain.
My body, my mind and my soul are in pain.
I no longer believe that my soul will be saved
As my mind feels bound and I feel betrayed.
If anyone is listening, please hear my cries
As he who jumps so often dies.
The edge is close now, I see over the line
The link between reason and despair are so fine.
If only I knew of a reason to stay
I might find it in me to start a new day -
With a smile on my lips and my spirit in flight
My heart full of love and a reason to fight.
To restore the damage in those I deceived, and
To act on my instincts and in what I believe.

Chrissi

CREATIVELY COMPOSED

Poetry is written by the imaginative mind,
From many races, this you will find.
Composing poetry, it's a noble art,
Linking words to gladden the heart.
All manner of styles sought by many,
From particular author, to the verses of many.
No matter the theme, whatever the time,
Putting into words, poetry in rhyme.

John P Evans

THE COMPOSITION

Who knows why the rhyming fascinates
The simple beat of words creates
A new picture to the simple mind and rates
As none other in opening new gates

To forms or visions visited
On us, thematic voices enlisted
In a music of its own insisted
Framed in the lines and metre listed

A simple beat can keep the
Crowds in dance or happy glee
Seen in words or bright verse at least a smile see
For such is poetry.

John Amsden

DANGER ON A SUMMER'S DAY
(A true story)

Have you ever met a ferret in your kitchen?
It really is a most alarming sight.
I stood still on the spot transfixed with horror
And then let out a mighty squawk of fright.

The trouble is, it *was* such lovely weather;
The doors were open and the access free.
My toes were showing through my summer sandals;
The ferret looked at them in heartfelt glee.

The tiny tots were safely in the garden.
They'd come to visit Grandma for the day;
But when they heard the screaming they came running
And squealed with joy this new-found friend to see.

By then he'd had a nibble at my trotters;
The feeling wasn't pleasant to my feet.
One bite can't do much damage to a grown-up,
But what if he'd moved on to tenderer meat?

I pushed the babies out into the garden
And grabbed a walking stick to chase him out.
No luck; he simply ran behind the oven
And then led me a dance all round about.

In case you think I really meant to harm him,
Let me at once set all your fears at rest.
I truly am a soppy mammal lover;
It's just the teeth that cause me some unrest.

Then Grandad came to help with my endeavour
And after arduous chase he met success.
He put that ferret in a box and closed it.
The ferret soon escaped, as you can guess.

To keep the toddlers safe he took them home then.
Their mummy roared with laughter when she heard,
I really can't think what's so very funny.
To mock at danger truly is absurd.

I closed the door and skulked inside in terror
Until my husband came back to my aid.
At last he put it in empty dustbin
And fixed the lid. This time inside he stayed.

From time to time we lifted up the cover
To check that he could breathe, and give him a drink,
He paid us back by leaping at our noses.
He didn't relish being in the clink.

At last the lady came from 'Ferret Rescue'.
She looked reproachful when she saw his plight.
She said 'Oh dear, he's nothing but a baby
And look how tame!' We did feel so contrite.

Carol Burton

LIFE

So there was a big bang
From which we all sprang -
That's what they tell us
Those clever fellers,

They tell us life begun
In some liquid dung
A chemical melting pot
That produced us lot.

Of course all this is very strange
But they tell us there was lots of change
From very fine particles
Came lots of different articles.

As they became more complex
They began to take different steps.
Eventually, you see,
They produced you and me.

Alan Holdsworth

THE CEDAR TREE

I saw a tree the other day
Its beauty took my breath away
Standing so tall nearly touching the sky
It made me stop and wonder why
We never see things as they really are
It's as if we are looking at some distant star
And wondering if there's life up there
And if there is do we really care
Things get so spaced out in the mind
If we dug deep what would we find
Who did create all this space and wonder
Was it designed or just some blunder
Did God create the Earth and sky
Then leave us all to wonder why
There doesn't seem to be much reason
Is it then the silly season
Or is it part of God's great plan
To find the worth of His creation . . . man.

June Clare

CRIME TIME

Oh what a torturous rhythm tick-tock
An instrument of pain is the prison clock
Tell me why do you march so agonisingly slow
Why don't you hurry so that I finally may go?
I know of my fate and I'm aware of my crime
So this time I spend waiting is my dying time
Your oddly paired hands read to signal my demise
And your expression is unchanging not like men's lives
Oh how I've wished you could be turned back
'Cause guilt tears at my heart more than any attack
You stare blankly at me, but I've no more tears to cry
Even if ancient tradition demands an eye for an eye
But one day my friend, just like in times long ago
You also won't be needed, people won't need to know
A calming peace will descend, the great rush will subside
Your march will be halted and no tears will be cried
But I know that I'm guilty it was proved beyond doubt
Aah! The hangman is ready; this is where I clock out.

Michael Bellerby

COMFORT

Come to me, come to me,
Softly touch my hair.
Come to me, come to me,
Although no eyes can see
I know that you are there.
Come to me, come to me,
When in my solitude
I feel you near,
To comfort me my dear.

Come to me, come to me,
Although I'm now alone,
We're not divided in our worlds,
Our love still makes us one.
So come to me, oh come to me,
Our love eternally to share,
To comfort me, to comfort me.
For deep within my heart
I know that you are there.

Jill M Kimber

CATS

A ginger ball of fur
He's curled up on my knee
How could anyone not love him
Certainly not me.
The other one is cream
With eyes of brilliant blue,
The hunt together as a team
God knows why I had two!
They bring me mice and birds and frogs
That squeal and jump and hop,
They think they're bringing love gifts
But I wish that they would stop,
I love the company they give me
Their presence keeps me sane,
When once you've had a cat friend
Life never is the same.

Joan Gray

SUNSHINE PRINCESS

Our sunshine Princess
With a heart full of grace,
A serene and lovely
Smile on her face,
Touching young children
Frail and infirm,
Showing a beautiful
Thoughtful concern,
Shaking hands with the sick
Others would not touch,
Transcending all ages
Her care was such.

We said our goodbyes
On a day the sun shone,
To our beloved Princess
From our lives now gone,
Behind her she left
A gift we can share,
To love one another,
And show that we care.

Brenda Hope Bethell

To Brenda

Time, friendless, pauses for the dead,
And wraps you in her bosom at the last.
And all the things you were, and felt, and said,
Have taken solemn shelter in the past.

Love, wisely, settles with you now,
And frees you from the pain and hurt and grief.
And all the loves you've known and held, somehow
Are lying silent in a wreath.

Life always puzzled you, I feel,
And lets you now depart this vale in light.
And truths and wide things that you knew were real,
Have gone with you into the night.

Anne Rolfe-Brooker

14TH FEBRUARY

Through shining days and shadowed weather
As I love you now I'll love you forever.

So, listen to your heart and come to me,
We'll be as birds in the sweet plum tree.
I'll sweep you to the vaults of an azure sky,
To the topmost cliffs where the eagles fly.

I'll cover you in gold from the autumn leaves,
And jewels from the seven glittering seas.
I'll steal you silver from the moon's white light
And perfume from the warmth of a summer's night.

You can bathe in the softest April showers,
Be clothed in a wealth of silken flowers,
Dance over rainbows, on the waves of the sea,
If you listen to your heart and come to me.

As I love you now so I'll love you forever
Through shining days, through shadowed weather.

G Howarth

To Show The Way

Long time ago, in a land faraway,
A stranger came amongst us, but could not stay.
The life he led, was simple, honest and loving too,
The message he left, to your own self be true.
Do onto others, as you would have done by,
Don't judge without checking, the stone in your own eye.
Reach out to all who are suffering and sad,
Help where you can, to make them feel glad.
Then the stranger's life has not been in vain,
'Cause the legacy he left was to help all in pain.
His teachings have continued, down through the ages,
Through prophets and priests, and wise old sages.

Audrey Walker

C'EST LA VIE

Negative words are all I hear
Negative people always near
Telling me just what to do
But my life wasn't made for you
So give me space, let me grow
And then in time that's when I'll show
That I am stronger than you think
When my world's crushed I will not shrink
I'll stand up and I'll show that I
Can be knocked down but I won't cry
I'll fall in love and be let down
But there'll be no tears; there'll be no frown
I'll make mistakes but don't we all
Yet I'll get up each time I fall
Just as the stars come out each night
Each time I'm hurt I'll stand and fight
And as I stand at death's door
Knowing I can fight no more
You'll see a smile upon my face
Because in my heart I will embrace
The times I've had, the times I've shared
With all the people for whom I've cared
Knowing that I did my best
It's then I'll lay my head to rest.

Fionnuala Faulkner

MAY DAY

May Day is a festival that is many centuries old.
It started back in Roman times, or so the story's told.
It heralds from the rites to Flora, Roman god of flowers.
They would dance for her to, once again, invoke her magic powers.

They danced in jubilation at the coming of the spring,
at the advent of the warmer days and all that they would bring.
The Northern European folk caught on to the idea
before it crossed the Channel and was developed over here.

In eighteen eighty-nine the communists took a hand,
millions of working people were not dependant on the land.
So now in many countries it is a national labour day
but in England it's a festival in the traditional way.

A maypole is erected with coloured streamers hanging down.
The May Queen is selected and she has a floral crown.
The revellers take the streamers and round the pole they dance.
To watch the colours intertwine could leave you in a trance.

In recent years it's taken a new lease of life somehow
but it's mostly young schoolchildren who celebrate it now.
Still, if some of them remember what the festival's about
they will probably make sure this old tradition won't die out.

T Ingram

TIME HAS NO RECOMPENSE

Time has no recompense
For the ungrowing in their finite sense;
The scarless children find the teeming day
A dream where their reality has to play.
But the storm-tides come, the rain
That washes wisdom in the tangled grain;
And the scarred ones rise, pitted with pain that is
Home for vision and metamorphosis.

Pamela Constantine

WEATHER FORECAST

You know that optimistic chap
Who stands in front of the weather map
What he engagingly foretells
Are scattered showers and sunny spells

The anticyclones come and go
The pressure may be high or low
But still he stands and still he dwells
On scattered showers and sunny spells

Fronts warm and cold go sailing by
But which are wet and which are dry
His answer like a peal of bells
Scattered showers and sunny spells

And when a cyclone hits our shores
Loud and fierce the tempest roars
Above the hurricane he yells
Scattered showers and sunny spells

D Sheasby

IGNORANT DESIRE

Your green-banked river
forms again and flows.
I water at a hole
where no grass grows

and in that thirsting
fever grope your land
only to find parched bones
in dust and sand.

You have a self
my needless self could know,
but through my ignorant
desire you go

a mere ghost of possession.
Which is true?
Need of your body
disembodies you.

Norman Buller

MY BABE

Thirteen pounds of pure delight
Thirteen pounds that wake me each night
She looks at me with eyes so blue
Without my babe what would I do
This little life so soft and warm
To her I'd never do no harm
A purer love there'll never be
Than the love my babe gives to me.

Irene Hanson

SONNET

Astrologers who nightly read the skies
Hope not to beckon down a charm of stars,
The striving, not th'attainment, is their prize,
Which, since Time fears it not, he never mars.
So spin the silver circles of the night,
Aloof, supreme and silent in their pride,
The watchers, whose possession is but sight,
They answer not, neither do they deride.
Then let me love, that have not hope nor fear,
And be you constant in inconstancy,
For should a star, or you, approach too near,
The world, and mine own eyes, would blinded be;
Then move not from thy sphere but to destroy,
And love me not - lest my heart fail with joy.

M A Sproat

HIGHER CHOICES

Soften me nature
Fill me with rapture,
Help me to surrender
Teach me to be tender.
These waves that break
Decisions I make,
All come down to me
What I want to be.

Where sweet rivers flow
Where scented gardens grow,
That is where you'll find me
Carried by each vision I see.
Knowing what I know now
Making right choices somehow,
Controlling my thoughts at last
My dreams will come to pass.

Standing still in this place
Every location has a trace,
Of what has gone before
Opening of a secret door.
What I am today
Will lead to a better way,
Love is all there is
Want to taste that sweet kiss.

My thoughts flying high
Seek no reasons why,
These moments in time
Embracing them, they are mine.
Taking time for reflection
Thinking through my direction,
Gentle are those voices
Leading me to higher choices.

Ian Barton

THE DAISY FIELD

The joys of nature captivating, never-ending,
And there's a simple pleasure each new year will yield.
The day is fair and there's a summer breeze attending,
- We'll take the dogs and see how fares the daisy field.

The lazy summer sounds dispelling worldly cares,
We savour rustic joys to city folk denied,
Then rounding corner we are taken unawares
By joie-de-vivre and loveliness personified.

For there across the field like stars you boldly drift,
Your pure simplicity so pleasing to the eye.
Bewitched, we drink our fill of nature's dazzling gift -
Your stunning impact underneath a summer sky.

With artless charms ensuring I'll return each year to see,
You have ensnared me and have cast your daisy spell on me.

Molly Read

MY MAN

In here alone, confused and sad of heart
Wondering why, oh why, did we have to part
A phone call away, yet I sit here and stare
Do you, can you, will you care?

The sun is shining, but my heart is black
How long before I go running back?
The nights are long, but the talking's not
Passions we knew are now forgot.

We have a child, an unforgettable bond,
You held us so close, you were so fond
Then came the rows, the lies, the deceit
Just when I thought our love was complete.

Let's get together and start afresh
Trials and tribulations, oh let us confess
We'll stay together, through all these things
Clasping hands, we'll see what life brings.

E Corr

TELL ME

Tell me of your darkest night my sweet,
For I shall be a lantern to your feet.

You cannot climb this silent hill alone,
Your broken heart beneath a standing stone.

Tell me of this grave,
Wherein now lies that love of life, so lost,
Within your eyes.

Roger Mosedale

WHOM THEN SHALL I FEAR?

Along life's way I tread,
  Getting older year by year,
But at my side I have my Lord -
  Whom then shall I fear?

Sometimes I cautiously proceed,
  Uncertainty takes hold -
And then I ask my God for help,
  His strength doth make me bold.

Along life's way I tread,
  Getting older year by year,
But at my side I have my Lord -
  Whom then shall I fear?

When hesitant at what to do,
  I turn to the one at my side,
And know that whatever the difficulty -
  God will help me in safety abide.

Along life's way I tread,
  Getting older year by year,
But at my side I have my Lord -
  Whom then shall I fear?

The time I spend weighing the pros and cons,
  Which path to take on life's way?
When all I need is to take the hand
  That guides me from day to day.

Along life's way I tread,
  Getting older year by year,
But at my side I have my Lord -
  Whom then shall I fear?

Lord grant me the strength to be true to Thee,
  No matter how hard that may be,
So that at life's end I may still remain,
  With Thee in perfect harmony.

Along life's way I tread,
  Getting older year by year,
But at my side I have my Lord -
  Whom then shall I fear?

Jean C Pease

MARTHA

My lassie, Martha, true Highland maid,
Will her proud memory ever fade?
Daily his words never ceased to flow
As Scotland's breezes o'er bracken blow,
For the Campbell clan ran high, blue blood,
That never another clan so stood,

Her suitors she had many,
But Martha had not any,
No love, nor marry,
Tom Dick or Harry!

A president knew her skill,
A principal knew her will,
Conscientious was she,
Clicked typing keys so free.

Laughter at party Christmas wash-up,
Disappeared Martha with towel and cup,
Crash! Breathing! Exit down cellar stairs,
Blamed, wide-open door for many tears.

Trips to hospital's good treatment,
Ankle hot-cold bathing frequent,
Water soothed her each night,
Washed to ease all her fright.

Our friendship grew,
Each treatment anew,
Cemented now,
But why and how?

Her days shone with jollity,
Surpassing all frivolity,
Dear Martha mine, for loyalty,
Wait heaven's good time for royalty.

Alice Blackburn

TONGUE IN CHEEK

It's not so easy when you're getting old;
You can't move fast enough to keep out the cold.
Winter takes its toll, and your joints all creak,
But your tongue's okay, and you can still speak.
It'll be no joke if that starts to rust;
It's always been there, the friend you can trust.
It's been there to help you tell a tall tale;
All these years, I've never known it to fail.
Sometimes, it's said things that weren't very nice;
I'm sure that was only just once or twice.
It's always been there when you've laughed or cried;
It's said the right things when a friend has died.
It's moved with your lips in all the right ways.
I hope it will work 'til the end of your days.

Geraldine Parr

MY WORK PLACE

My work, what a place

People leaving without
A trace

Not enough time to know
Their face

What have people got
Against this place?

Look at us we've been here
Years

Sometimes it does bring
You close to tears

There used to be plenty
Of cheer

But it's gone down over the
Years

Maybe one day there will be
Plenty more cheer.

Leeanne Shires

RHYMING VERSES APPEAL IN SIMPLE STYLE

I feel rhyming verse is so expressive to read;
You can visualise the beauty of your subject indeed.
Beauty of the seasons, or of nature all around,
The tragedy of disaster, and words of comfort to be found.
The shock of bereavement and thoughtful words there,
Be a true friend and show that you care.
An enjoyable holiday, of fine scenery and views,
Or of historical splendour; whichever you choose.
The admiration you have for a friend, good and true,
Or a noted personality who inspires you.
Just make your words simple, but very sincere,
And your message in rhyme should appear very clear!

Marjorie Cowan

SPOKEN WORDS

What words we speak,
Convey meanings.
It reaches all our inner feelings.
Findings of true selves in thee,
Creates a new person in me!
It hurts those lies, they tell to thee.
It hurts those lies, the believence of me.
Are you deaf, don't you hear!
All of this heartache,
Is my tears.
Are you blind, don't you see!
I am a human being,
Yes all of me.

Jenifer Ellen Austin

THE WAY TO PEACE

You hear the news on the TV or radio,
Of violence and wars unleashed;
Of murder and muggings wherever you go,
You wonder, 'Is there a way to peace'.

Some wars are caused by the colour of skin,
The white man not liking the black;
Others are caused by power-mad men,
For to rule all the world is their track.

Murder and muggings are mostly for greed,
With people coveting what they have not;
They're jealous of what they don't really need,
Because all they really need is God.

There are also wars that are caused by religion,
In which all people should be ashamed;
For just stop and think, whatever denomination,
The God that we worship is the same.

Jesus once said that you should love,
Your neighbour as yourself;
No matter the colour, they're sent from above,
They all rely on God's help.

So if we could learn to love one another,
Whatever their colour or creed;
Then we'd all start to live like sister and brother,
I think that's the way to peace.

Reg Cook

TEN WORDS

One bad word that's spoken in haste,
Can upset a person and cause disgrace;
Two people together kneeling in prayer,
Can find the answer to problems they share.

Three rich men with hearts so pure,
Can raise the standards of the poor;
Four young girls as sweet as can be,
Can make four boys live happily.

Five days make up a working week,
With a clear conscience you'll be able to sleep;
Six days, God said, thou shalt labour,
So do your best to follow our Saviour.

Seven is the day that you should rest,
It is the Sabbath that the Lord blessed;
Eight is the time when all good children,
Should be in their bed, that's not a problem.

Nine out of ten lepers that our Lord cured,
Didn't even thank Him, that's for sure;
Ten is the commandments that God gave to us,
Follow them faithfully, and in Him you can trust.

Thelma Cook

DIANA

The fanfare of a hunting horn, faint and far away;
a figure, distant in the dawn, charms the newborn day -
Diana, goddess of the chase, in radiant attire,
fills with light each shadowed place, the crowding hills afire
with those who follow in her wake and slyly touch her hem,
press those private griefs that ache beneath her diadem.

Her coterie admire and fawn; she's patient and demure;
wounded by the critics' scorn all goddesses endure
and, when she gives her cast-off gowns for charity to sell,
ignores the hardened cynics' frowns and twisted tales they tell -
cheap gossip-monger-tabloid talk, the cutting words that flay,
while paparazzi cameras stalk the huntress viewed as prey.

They gather - savage sycophants - as vultures pick at bones,
but what, on her, looked elegant with classic overtones,
hangs empty on the auction rail - a rare, discarded skin,
the spirit flown; the fabric pale; the magic wearing thin . . .
A few might fancy in the folds a trace of perfume clings,
although the scent has long grown cold, they rummage
                                        through her things.

While decoys keep the hounds amused, she flees the social scene,
abandoning her royal blues for sporty hunting green -
Diana, doyenne of le chic, the smart set imitates
the look, the gracious smile technique her public life dictates . . .
In dreams she rides romantic fields, still longing to possess
the quarry that remains concealed - elusive happiness.

J M Harvey

PASSING A HOME-MADE BAKER'S SHOP!

Nothing makes us think of home,
Like smells of homely cooking!
Bread, pies or roasting meat,
Send us homeward, drooling!

Close your eyes, 'taste' the smells,
In your mind, you are back home!
Mother, apron-clad, stands there,
Apple pie? Why did I roam!

An overwhelming homesickness,
Makes you want to weep!
You hurry on with other thoughts,
On appointments you must keep!

Somewhere in your inner self
Those smells just linger on!
You go home and write a letter
Long overdue - to Mum!

Of all our senses, it is smell
That can be the most provocative!
For of all the good things in our life,
It is, the most evocative!

Evelyn Mary Eagle

SERENITY

You are rare and so admirable
I have a longing for you and find you desirable
If I could have you in my life
I'd have so much less trouble and strife
I sometimes see you in someone else's eyes
But you evade me and it's no surprise
To see me rant and rave
It's no way to behave
You I want so much of - oh yes plenty
Just think how wonderful that would be - serenity

Carey Sellwood

THE BOOKS

Silently standing there in rows
Upon a high shelf thick with dust,
Up where the smoke cloud drifts and flows,
Unread, unnoticed, it's unjust.

For these are books, and long ago
Their authors toiled to pages fill,
Oft working by a candle's glow
With bottled ink and goose's quill.

Up there among them we could find
Tales told by long forgotten men,
Or wisdom coming from the mind
Of one who wields the mighty pen.

These precious words the authors chose
To make their meaning very clear
Now stand in sad neglected rows
Where people drink their lager beer.

Mervyn S Whale

THE DALES AND THE LAKES

The beauty of the British countryside is a sight to see,
The Dales and Lakes are the places I like to be.
In the Dales the three peaks, fate decided that's where we went,
Ingleborough, Whernside and Peny Ghent.

Going up Peny Ghent so few people around,
The stillness in the air, silence abound.
In the silence, the omniscient presence I could feel,
The pressures of life, this certainly would heal.

Visiting the Lake District gave me much pleasure,
Walking the fells at my time and leisure.
The mountains around are a wonderful sight,
On Pavy Arc you can view the Langdales from a great height.

On Helvelyn a steady climb to the top,
Will the beautiful sights ever stop.
Clambering up Great Gable through long paths of scree,
I found a memorial of two great wars, this was the place I wanted
to see.

Bowfell and Pike of Bliscoe are two we decided to climb
Climbing these mountains gave me great joy, it was sublime.
The years have flown by, now I have become older
Seeing these mountains in their grandeur, now I'm just a beholder.

Robert Baslington

DREAM POEM

There are quiet places; vales of silver flowers
Thin-spun with gossamer lit by moonbeams,
Sweet petals wafted down in swirling showers;
Calm crystal lakes and clear bird-haunted streams;
Deep thickets where the glow-worm's green lamp gleams
And in the dusk the fireflies flicker by,
Dart through the balmy summer air which seems
To drift with dreams from regions of the sky
While past tall dark-branched trees the snow-white night owls fly.

In the cool dawn the encircling clouds unfold
Round magic palaces, domed softest blue,
Dim silvery walls all woven-in with gold
And little stars that shine like beads of dew.
Strange birds, rich-plumed, of deepest emerald hue
On glittering wings about the high dome glide,
While strains of heavenly music wander through
Calm as on windless nights the swelling tide
When over gleaming rocks low rollers, moonlit, slide.

Oh world mysterious; mystery of dreams,
Of lands unknown beyond an unclimbed height,
Of music from the sea and mountain streams,
Of silent stars whose song is past the night,
Of all the changing colours of the light
When breezes blow the early mist away;
World with your dreams as brief as rainbows bright
Though on a rainbowed shore still children play;
The wonder is the dreams will never fade away.

Diana Momber

AW, BUT SIR...

Awesome spectacle, or God awe-full mess?
What part did Xena, Warrior Princess
Play in the history of Ancient Greece?
She never helped search for the Golden Fleece!
You're more inspired by Ray Harryhausen
Than Homer, unless it's Homer Simpson
You have uppermost in your tiny mind.
Just for the record I think you will find
That Virgil was a poet, not the pilot
Of Thunderbird Two, and you're talking rot
From start to finish so why don't you go
To the library, not the video
Shop section on sword and sandal epics.
Old Steve Reeve's movies are not biopics.
Forgive me for sounding a little rude
Your work's awesome in its ineptitude
For an academic dissertation.
Rewrite it now without hesitation.
Read the damn books. Don't watch old films instead.
Put all thoughts of Xena out of your head.
I know it's a labour of Hercules
But I want this essay for Monday please.

Arthur Chappell

THE SOLDIER

If my life should pass away, in some foreign land
Just think of me as English still, and try to understand
In that small plot, all England is distilled
Her thoughts, her ways, her flowers, forever stilled
In silent prayer, for England and her shores
Her tinkling streams and flooded rivers roar
And think this heart as pure as new born babe
Far from England in some foreign soil laid
Has played a part in England's happy days and peaceful ways
You are at peace, your children's laughter sounds and joy abounds.

Dora Watkins

LOOKING FOR INSPIRATION

She looks towards him for inspiration,
But no great comment does he ever make.
How she longs for a deep conversation,
But the deafening silence he'll not break.

Again she longs for an explanation,
Please speak to me she wails, for goodness sake.
Silent he remains in contemplation,
She's left wondering what action to take.

S Mullinger

MOBILE PHONE FEVER

Dan is walking along
In the street, through the throng,
To his ear does he hold a receiver.
In the mouthpiece he speaks
And an answer he seeks,
All a sign of some mobile phone fever.
'Is that Stan? This is Dan,
What a chat, see old man,
To be passing the time this fine morning.
As I'm going through town,
Some poor folk seem to frown,
Think they must be in some sort of mourning.'
Then he hears a strange voice,
One that does not rejoice,
So, Stan must have a guest, he's surmising.
Comes a sudden tirade,
With some anger displayed,
To Dan, it is all most surprising.
'Now young man, I'm not Stan,
Hear me out, if you can,
You must know that you rang the wrong number.
I've been working all night,
So it just isn't right,
You have woken me up from my slumber.'
In the meantime, the sound,
By some people around,
In the street, is found to be disturbing.
So when using his phone
Some more care should be shown,
As he makes much less noise, with more curbing.

D J Price

THE HUMAN GAME

The world is covered with darkness,
With shadows roaming the land.
The world was left up to us,
In fate of human hand.

To play with its emotions,
We were never really told.
This world was not a toy,
We've left it stale and cold.

The world is covered with darkness.
We've always turned our blind eyes,
On the hope and dreams of light,
Now, as we look up to burnt skies.

With pollution, poison, lies and mistrust,
We turned the world on its head,
With death, destruction, losers and sin,
For all of the tears the world's shed.

The world is covered with darkness,
We should return from whence it came,
We have no idea how to cope with this,
Playing the human's game.

With atomic bomb and nuclear war,
All of which are manmade.
Throw away all maps and blueprints,
Before we all begin to fade.

Jamie Barnes

FLIGHT

Do you ever wonder why?
Although the birds were given wings to fly
Man he had to do the same
By inventing the frightful aeroplane
And in so doing he changed my life
By filling it with fear and strife
Each year when holidays come round
I'm thinking of having to leave the ground
Off to the docs I have to go
For pills to make my heart beat slow
And when I manage to climb on board
I sit and wait for the engine's roar
Eyes shut tight and knuckles white
As like the birds we take to flight
And, no matter what they may say
It's never natural to travel this way
We reach a height at which we cruise!
Where a small bit of my fear I lose
The drinks come round and people prattle
While I am listening for every rattle
The captain tells us our height and speed
And I think to myself 'That's all I need'
Can't leave my seat no matter what I do
There's no way I could make it to the loo
A couple of hours is all I can stand
And then we have to prepare to land!
I clutch the arms as we go down
Praying safely to reach the ground
We land quite well in sudden thrust
And joy comes on me in euphoric rush
We've reached our holiday destination
But I'd still rather go from a railway station!

Valerie Hillier

THE RELUCTANT HEIR

Why this bout of caprice,
this flounce of defiance,
can there be any substance,
in his stated reluctance,
and pure indifference,
to pursue his inheritance.

And have we no assurance,
that this fit of impudence,
which has tried our endurance,
won't meet with his persistence.

All we have is discordance,
and harmonic imbalance,
which is causing much turbulence,
through his thorough ignorance.

His actions were at variance,
with a look that was jaundice,
as he covered some distance,
and forged his disappearance.

Jean Paisley

MYSTERY MAN

He was a queer looking bloke,
Said he'd come from 'up above',
Complained he'd lost all his folk
And was now bereft of love.

He did not know this strange place,
Had never been here before,
Mumbled about aerospace,
Wondered what was a 'seashore'.

He was dressed in cap and gown,
With a face as pale as ash,
Showing a permanent frown,
Talked a lot of balderdash.

Suddenly he disappeared,
Leaving clothes upon the ground,
Regretfully we all feared,
He had now become earthbound.

Eric Allday

NEWNESS OF SPRING

Walking down a lovely little lane,
Where flowers and blossoms blaze again.
Birds in hedgerows building their nests,
Collecting twigs and grass no one ever rests.

Some build high in the tall treetops
Others are using disused chimney pots
Spring is here, earth's no longer a frosty white,
Hope pervades the newness to the light.

In the meadows sheep with lambs so sweet,
Swans build where the river and stream meet.
From winter's darkness new life is born,
And it's also brighter in the early morn.

Margaret Upson

MOTHER

To see your picture on the page,
Takes me back to another age,
To when we children needed care,
Mother dear, you were always there.

You kept our home so shining bright,
Our lives were always full of light,
No trouble was too much for you,
You loved your youngsters through and through.

But woe betide us if we dare,
Be rude or cheeky anywhere,
Down came your hand upon our leg,
And your pardon we had to beg.

Chores aplenty we had to do,
You knew many a thing or two
About what life for us would be,
So you moulded us tenderly.

Many a year has passed my dear,
But it seems that you're always near,
Guiding and helping all of us,
Just as you did - without a fuss.

Isobel Crumley

TWYNHOLM GREETINGS CARD

'Tis Miss Janet Charters' birthday today you see
Hence a card from Jean and me.
On front of card, there is a cat, I bet.
It is expecting some meal to get.
The cat is along with us with zest.
To wish you yourself Jay, all the best.
We want no feed,
There is no need
On this day Thursday,
Third of May.
Zero one, which makes your anniversary
Eighty-one, so Jay, on this your birthday,
We both have this to say,
You have made the eighth decade,
An' congratulations, you lovely maiden.

George Theodore Harrison

THE BRIDGE WHICH DIVIDES

On wrong side of Craigavon Bridge,
where bile flows from Tullyally,
these nightmares creep as hoar from fridge
in an eerie, swirling ballet.

Where bile flows from Tullyally
with the hate-fog from Newbuildings,
in an eerie swirling ballet
timid murderers are milling.

With the hate-fog from Newbuildings,
drugged by a blind ferocity,
timid murderers are milling,
devising next atrocity.

Drugged by a blind ferocity,
complacent in their mystery;
devising next atrocity,
these monsters live in history.

Complacent in their mystery,
with 'Butcher's Apron' as a cloak
these monsters live in history -
on reality afraid to choke.

With 'Butcher's Apron' as a cloak
they slink remorseless and uncouth -
on reality afraid to choke -
to silence those who speak the truth.

They slink remorseless and uncouth -
these nightmares - creep as hoar from fridge
to silence those who speak the truth
on wrong side of Craigavon Bridge.

Perry McDaid

YOU TOUCH MY HEART

When you're in a dream, a yesterday's haze
Thoughts are captured, the meeting was made
You touched my heart, in a flash you were gone
I did not want to part, what have you done?
Fate for sure it has to be, is this really our destiny?
I've waited so long for time with you
Not to blow it, tell me you to
Relaxing the nerves you make me feel
Tender, surrender moments to steal
Spilling my drink and feeling a mess
We look, we talk, and we jest.
For time to stand still we have so much to say
My love time's gone, until another day
Eyes catch, then snatch, that moment disappears
Like a puff of smoke the haze appears.
Thoughts of adventure we both have planned
Look the time glass empties its sand.
Lost in the spell we crossed in flight
My dreams are only of you tonight
When will I see you again?
I cannot stand this pain anymore.
My love do you feel the same?
It's you I've been looking for.
Is this really our destiny?
Fate for sure it has to be,
What have you done?
I didn't want to part,
In a flash you were gone
You touch my heart.

Anne Joyce Farley

SEVEN DAYS
(To Nathan)

Seven days drag on so long,
Seven days you have been gone.
I miss helplessly looking in your eyes
This time away from you I despise.

I see you outside of work
You come over and talk to me.
I smile politely but inside I'm sad
I dream of you kissing me.

I can't wait until I see you again
To stop this forlorn pain.
I view from afar waiting to see
If you will notice me.

We went to your friend's house
We had a good time
Laughing and joking, the two of us
With your make-up on you looked fine.

I watch you work, pack your crisps
I dream about kissing your lips.
I want you to hold me tight in your arms
And write lovely notes onto your palms.

I want to label you with my love
And never let you go.
I want to be with you all the time,
The way I feel I want you to know.

Jodie McKane

A POEM FOR ME

A poem for me must have rhythm and rhyme,
With a swinging-skirt lilt and toe-tapping time,
With none of these, it's just arranged prose,
As easy to write as blowing your nose.

Beat out a rhythm with words and phrases,
Sort out a rhyme that deserves praises,
Give me a poem to get my teeth into,
That will seem like a dance to get my feet in too.

We can expound over beauty beheld in a dream,
But without rhythm, it's just not my scene,
We can muse about lovers, with passion and fire,
But without rhyme, it's not my desire.

Plover

THE TRUE ENTITY OF LIFE

Daybreak! And the sun shines through
She warms the land with golden hue
The land, still sleepy, shudders slightly
As beams on tiptoe, nimble, sprightly

Make their way across the grass
Sprinkling dewdrops is their task.
The moon now faded gives a smile
At least he now can sleep a while.

The waking state of humankind
In various moods to greet the day
Determines how the sun will shine
To let her in or block her way.

When we are open to all things
We feel ourselves to be connected
We feel the pulse of life that brings
A love to tell we're not rejected.

To guide us, help us through the day
Knowing life is but a play
The choice is ours to do our part
Each thought creates a brand new start.

So be responsive to yourself
Look inwards, tap your inner force
Feel the love that wants to help
Don't focus on regret, remorse!

Until it dawns within our minds
And crustiness gets left behind
That we and nature all are one
We are the light, the love, the sun.

Through faith we come to really know
As life itself we're here to grow!

Lorenza Cangiano

HEAD COLD

Somewhere cold, the letters find a stage for words to dance,
Sentencing their paragraphs to act like Kings of France.

In the blue, the writers fly, so eager for the script.
In the mind, intelligences die, like John Doas in the crypt.

Search, you thinkers out of time, must you join the pact?
How do angels on the screen learn the missing act?

Diaries burst with winning ways, so the story goes.
Open tales and anecdotes fuel the sparkling shows.

But you're missing what you have. You've misunderstood.
There's no mystery in this dome. It dwells within your blood.

Now you know how old you seem in theatres of speech.
Use your characters, bold, unleashed - but hesitate to teach!

Look, the writer isn't sage, how his tears have wept.
Test his crestfallen energies. Upon you, how they've crept.

Encores litter where they lie, on boards empowered trapped.
Bills can't figure only yours; while others' hopes are zapped.

Heed the warning, feed the need, don't imply you're dead.
You have all the silvered wine, right there in your head.

S Pete Robson

ORANG YAWNING

What is in that yawn
that I cannot see?
A dream, a feeling,
a passing fantasy?
Resting from swinging
around through the trees.
Scratching and yawning
whilst picking for fleas.

K Axon

DON'T

Don't lean so near,
I'm not listening
To those whispers
In my ear.

Don't let me feel
Your breath upon my face.
I think we both should
Give ourselves some space.

Don't hold me close
The way I want you to.
We each have partners
There are things we mustn't do.

Don't look at me that way,
This is goodbye,
And it pains me so, to see
A grown man cry.

Joyce Walker

THE LOST GENERATION
(Aberfan, 1966)

Today, the little town lies still
In sleek new lines beneath a sun
That smiles benevolently on
The triumph of a job well done.

And now, in cubes of brick and glass,
Fresh promise stands in sharp relief,
Untroubled by the stigma of
Disaster, with its buried grief.

And business runs from day to day,
Unhindered by its sombre past,
For no one now dare contemplate
The old, demented trumpet blast.

But once the demon furies raged
In furnace fear, and crushed the life
From maidenhood, while time-worn truths
Succumbed to Mammon's whetted knife.

Volcanic terror hurled its wrath
Like brimstone on a hapless town,
And slaughtering sweet innocence,
Brought half a generation down.

And empty were those slate-grey streets
In mourning for a childhood lost,
When *dies ire* anguish forced
A nation to repent the cost.

But that was centuries ago!
Today, the little town lies still,
And consciences compliantly
Remember but with half a will.

S H Smith

THE CLOCK HANDS

I watched the second hand on the clock
Moving quickly around its face
The minute hand moved more slowly
The hour hand had given up the race

'Let's race against the clock,' said second hand
Minute hand said, 'Race against time'
Hour hand more sedately uttered
'Let's co-ordinate and make the thing chime.'

Second hand spinning, barely saw the figures
Minute hand studied where he'd been
Hour hand surveyed the figures thoroughly
And considered what went on inbetween

The hands continuing in their circuits
Found that each upon the other depends
Learning the names of the figures they passed
Increasing their circle of friends

John Remmington

JUST WATCHING

Watching the birds in the trees,
Or them feeding on the ground,
With their different antics,
Much pleasure can be found.

You watch with amazement,
How quickly they can fly,
Land or take off in a moment,
Just a twinkling of an eye.

The robins and the blackbirds,
Keep their own territory,
Just like the squirrel,
As he leaps from tree to tree.

Looking at the rabbits,
They may be very sweet,
But a quick slap on the concrete,
Sends them somewhere else to eat.

Then there is the pheasant,
Who taps on the patio door,
Asking for his morning snack,
Then later returns for more.

So spend some time watching,
See these marvels all for free,
Remember 'God' has put them there,
For everyone to see.

Will A Tilyard

FULFILLMENT

When all around is darkness,
When all dangers are unseen,
Be grateful for your blindness
Sparing you what could have been.
Where no one hears a word you say,
No matter how hard you shout,
Remember it has always been this way
And that they will work it out.
When you see a tree about to fall
And your efforts cannot halt it,
Blame it not for doing what couldn't be done,
It is not for us to fault it,
When all your troubles could be undone
By being a wealthier man,
Focus your impotence into pride
For your life has gone to plan.
Even as your death approaches
And time's charger has his way,
Be not surprised for all men die
And who would truly wish to stay?
Leave immortality to the gods,
They and it deserve each other,
Remember your life and your uniqueness,
A flame even eternity cannot smother.

M Morris

YOU'LL NEVER WALK ALONE

You'll never walk alone my friend
Though oft it seems to be,
The path you tread seems full of woe
And gloom is all you see!
Though next when down your darkest path
Afraid and far from home,
Remember Jesus' words to you
'You'll *never* walk alone'!
For often when we're hurting
And no hope there seems to be,
The gentle words of Jesus come,
'Just trust, believe in *Me*'!
For only when we trust in *Him*
And with him heartaches share,
Can he then act on our behalf
Releasing us from care!
So friend, please don't despair
Or think you're *ever* on your own,
For once your trust is in God's son,
You'll *never* walk alone!

E S Dean

ONE STOLEN MOMENT

Her chastity belt locked up fast,
the young wife breathes a heavy sigh,
her lord and master gone at last,
watched from a turret slit on high.

On stockinged feet, she hurries down,
close to the wall so cold to touch,
holding tight the end of her gown,
free for now from his evil clutch.

Breathlessly she unlocks the door,
making sure that nobody sees,
softly calls as she's done before,
thinks of her love with trembling knees.

Her bedchamber safe from prying eyes,
at last he holds her in his arms
throwing off his servant's disguise,
excites her with his smiles and charms.

With trembling hands, using the key
he'd copied while her husband slept,
unlocks the belt to set her free,
drying her tears where she had wept.

The fire of youth burning brightly,
consumes them both, leaving them weak,
a last embrace, clinging tightly,
parting sorrow, they cannot speak.

A lingering kiss, then he rides
into the night lit by the moon,
cold iron clamped once more to her sides,
knows that her lord will be back soon.

A Odger

THE ODEON

I remember watching movies
At the Odeon in Leeds
With friends who were the soundtrack
Of my spiritual needs,
And in that picture palace
Of the sixties I began
To witness the perfection
That was idolised by man.

I remember smoking freely
In the darkness of my dreams
As movie stars compounded
My belief in many schemes,
And in the crowded silence
I could feel serenity
Encroach upon my thinking
For the film's entirety.

I remember each performance
On the massive silver screen
That energised emotions
With each scintillating scene,
And there were many lovers
Melting into works of art
Inside the heaving presence
Of a city's pulsing heart.

I remember how those movies
Left me feeling unconfined
And seemingly uplifted
In my overburdened mind,
But in the neon chaos
Life's reality kicked in
Amid the roaring traffic
And the crowd's incessant din.

I W Wade

. . . AND THEN WE DANCED

Across the sea of azure hue
Of dimmed lights' glow and smoky blue,
Of keen vibration's throb and beat
And sweet sensation's summer heat
With melted heart, I gazed at you.

And in that frozen moment too
You gazed at me as if on cue.
We each arose, our love complete
    And then we danced.

And thus we stayed the whole night through
As pulses raced and passions grew:
Unknown, the chance that we would meet
How you would sweep me off my feet
To world's uncharted pastures new,
    Where still we dance.

Jill Thompson Barker

UNFINISHED BUSINESS

You're there - I'm here
And seldom do we meet, my dear.
The love space keeping us apart
Is treasured in each other's heart.
Our feelings traverse many years
We never see the other's tears.
Our lives are but a distant twinship
Though thankfully without the kinship,
Inspiration to both at least,
Unfinished business - never ceased.
When to Elysian fields we flee
We'll be together - you and me.

Roma Scrivener

THROUGH THE EYES OF A CHILD

The minutely observed world of childhood
As seen through the eyes of the very small
Has seemingly limitless boundaries
Within the confines of the garden wall.

I explored my own Lilliputia,
Dwarfed by the rows of blooms as tall as trees,
And beyond the orderly a tangle
Of secret pathways resonant with bees.

I could spend ages watching a woodlouse
In its slow progression along the bank,
Or a snail gliding like a galleon
Over dead leaves which smelt pungently dank.

One evening as dusk began to fall
I lingered knowing it was time for bed.
I stood, mesmerised by the fading light
And the first faint stars pricking overhead.

The sky, a sequinned, vast black velvet void,
Held a mystery called infinity
Which burst on my developing senses
With sudden and breathtaking clarity.

A voice called from indoors, but still I stood
Savouring this moment, caught on the raw.
It dawned that I was but a speck in time
And the knowledge of it filled me with awe.

Rosina Winiarski

STORM

Oh restless sea on stormy day,
When Boreas and Neptune play,
The raging wind and breakers roar -
With frightening force, upon the shore.

The flying clouds across the sky -
Like Woden's warships sailing by;
Go scurrying past to tell the tale,
Of coming storm and rising gale.

The lightning's flash with blinding light
Like shining arrows gleaming bright,
With startling speed and wild array
To rent the sky across the bay.

Then - set the ragged crags alight
And bathe their spires in eerie light.
Like sentinels on castle's keep -
Their silent watch o'er foaming deep.

The hissing rain in torrents pours
Now mingling with the thunder's roars
Makes startled seabirds homeward flee
To sheltered crags from furious sea.

The swell upon its heaving breast
Like chariots - race with foaming crest
To meet the rocks - that bar the way
With deafening crash and blinding spray.

Majestic might, eternal force
Almighty power - is this the source
The great creator - from on high -
Who rules the earth, the sea, the sky.

Marjorie Lancaster

THE MOUSE

In Liverpool there stood a house,
And in it lived a wily mouse.
Never caught. He'd too much nous!
This time-defying little scouse.

But then one lovely summer's day,
Shortly after he'd hit the hay,
He woke to hear something at play,
Very near to where he lay!

Then there came a funny sound,
His heart was thundering, he found.
Something was near him on the ground,
And it was soft, and warm, and round!

And such a noise! What could it be?
Instinct told the mouse to flee.
Yet - 'I'm a mighty mouse,' said he,
He'd never met a cat you see!

'Oh foolish mouse,' Miaowed Tom the cat,
'You're not as clever as all that.
In fact you really are a prat.'
And with a paw he squashed it flat . . . !

Barbara Bradley

A Ghost Story

I know a big house called The Grange.
I worked there once; saw something strange:
I saw a gas man gas himself,
Then float through air onto a shelf!
I don't know how they got him down,
As I'd rushed to the Rose and Crown
To have a drink - Scotch on the rocks.
The barman said, 'Best thing for shock.
Now, tell me just what has occurred.'
I told him, though my voice was slurred.
He stared at me, quite at a loss,
And said, 'You'd better tell my boss.'
The landlord, seated on a chair,
Said, 'Gas men don't float through the air!'
But this one did. Now every night
His ghost gives people such a fright.
If you don't find this story strange,
Just spend the night outside The Grange
And let me know what you think then -
You'll not see me back there again!

Roger Williams

ANGELS IN BLACK STOCKINGS, PLEASE COME BACK

Though Florence Nightingale modernised
And recreated nursing's image,
She should tour wards now, and find much to chastise
The passing times for. How horrid to see
Black-stockinged angels look less womanly!
Instead of frocks, and aprons they wore then,
They've put on trews and tunics, like the men.

Nurses in my aunt Janet's time in Hove
Learned hands-on patient care through their three years
Of studentship, till qualified. All strove
To ease the pain and suffering, calm fears
Of hospital procedure, dry tears.
Now, ward hygiene is hopeless; bugs are back.
Florence would give subcontract staff the sack.

Gillian C Fisher

THE LAUGHING PHILOSOPHER

I am sure if he were alive today
The choice of the people, Democritos
Would laugh at the not so much démodé
Way some people think, as calamitous

He put his eager eyes out, it is said
So he could ponder, more deeply reflect
On the inanity of men who strayed
From the obvious, asserting 'We're correct'

One can only surmise what he would make
Of Homo sapiens' perversion
To alter nature, wildly undertake
With feeble pretexts, its demolition

As a speculative man of science
Seeing men, not even for knowledge, attempt
To follow with blind ovine obedience
Gods and trends, he'd laugh with utmost contempt

Being the exception that confirms the rule
In a city where reigned, proverbially
Stupidity, suffering every fool
He must have felt somewhat very lonely

The wise man of Abdera left his mark
For others to follow and prove their worth
Where are the persons today with a spark
Of intellect to match his thinking mirth?

J-C Chandenier

SUBMISSIONS INVITED
SOMETHING FOR EVERYONE

POETRY NOW 2001 - Any subject,
any style, any time.

WOMENSWORDS 2001 - Strictly women,
have your say the female way!

STRONGWORDS 2001 - Warning!
Age restriction, must be between 16-24,
opinionated and have strong views.
(Not for the faint-hearted)

All poems no longer than 30 lines.
Always welcome! No fee!
Cash Prizes to be won!

Mark your envelope (eg *Poetry Now) 2001*
Send to:
Forward Press Ltd
Remus House, Coltsfoot Drive,
Peterborough, PE2 9JX

OVER £10,000 POETRY PRIZES
TO BE WON!

Judging will take place in October 2001